FANTASVISS

The Short but not too Brief Tale of an Icelandic Spy in Switzerland

C.H. Roserens

© Cédric Henri Roserens

Éditions du Char-à-Thym

v24 .-. . --. ..- .-.. ..- ...

FOREWORD

This short tale is a small tribute to Switzerland, my homeland, seen from the eyes of a spy from Iceland, where I lived for six years. It is inspired by a train journey I did in 2007. I visited the 26 capital cities of the 26 Swiss cantons in just one week. The path of the protagonist is in all respects identical to mine, with the notable exception that it lasts one month rather than one week. The duration of the train rides can be found in the appendix. It is indeed closer to an informal guide to Switzerland than to a spy story. It is a fiction though. The politicians of the prologue and the epilogue, as well as the characters met by the hero, are imaginary. On the other hand, the historical and sports figures, the places, the cultural and culinary experiences are very real. The story takes place in 2017, five years after *Happísland*, a similar story starring a Swiss spy in Iceland (see the "Also by" section at the end of the book). The title, *Fantasviss*, comes from fantastic and *Sviss*, which means Swiss in Icelandic.

I wish you a pleasant reading experience!

to Walter Tell

PROLOGUE

Álftanes, Iceland, 20 April 2017

April 20 is a special day in Iceland. Named *Sumardagurinn fyrsti*, it is the first day of what they call summer. 2° Celsius, strong winds, heavy rain. They must be joking. Inside Bessastaðir, the Presidential residence, it is stormy too, and hot, hot and stormy in the heads. It has been three years since Switzerland came ahead of Iceland on top of Dubreuil's Ranking, the most reliable quality-of-life country ranking in the world. It is time for a change. Iceland wants to be number one again.

The cream of the crop of the Icelandic ministers is in the middle of a deep conversation with President Ragnar Gnarr Gnarrson in his Non-Oval Office. Among them Prime Minister Arndís Rós Björksdóttir, LGBT and Culture Minister Ævar Stein Kasperson, Fishery and Agriculture Minister Aðalgeir Gull Björnsson, as well as Football and Foreign Minister Margrét Olga Kristjánsdóttir. They are trying to understand how Switzerland has been able to overtake Iceland, in spite of the recent Icelandic successes in football and tourism that came as a relief after the harsh financial crisis of 2008 and the eruption of Eyjafjallajökull in 2010. Conclusion of the meeting: somebody has to go spy on Switzerland to see more clearly what it is they are doing better than Iceland and spot some weaknesses.

That somebody is Sigmundur Sig Sigmundsson, 44 years old, officially an employee of the LGBT and Culture Ministry, unofficially a VSA of the IVSS (a very special agent of the Icelandic Very Secret Services). IVSS is so secret that nobody knows about them in Iceland, apart from a few ministers and President Gnarrson. Sigmundur Sig Sigmundsson, code name Triple Sig, was among the guests in Bessastaðir. Familiar with secret missions abroad, he has been involved in the recent past in the Faroes, Shetland, Åland, and Äland. Nicknamed the Invisible Sig, he is the perfect match to spend a month unnoticed in Switzerland. Yes, one month. July 2017, to visit the 26 capitals of the 26 Swiss provinces, known as cantons. One day per capital. No more, no less. The budget is tight. One day to discover the delicacies of the town and canton, the interesting events going on, the lifestyle, the infrastructures, etcetera. A copious program to be repeated 26 times. A travel diary will be filled by Agent Triple Sig. It will be thoroughly analysed during the debriefing meeting in Bessastaðir on 15 August 2017.

Sigmundur Sig Sigmundsson's travel diary excerpts are to be read on the following 27 pages.

Geneva (GE) – 1 July 2017

Landing just before noon. The airport is very crowded. It is a Saturday and school holidays just started. Everybody is going away. I am going against the departing crowd. First impression: the public transport network is efficient. In less time than you need to swallow a shot of *brennivín*, I reach the city centre by train. I notice that a lot of people are in panic mode, glued to their smartphones. I can feel the tension and the worry hanging around. What the hell is happening? I ask the nearest guy. He tells me the cause of the panic: the direct train to Lausanne is 3 minutes late! He had to call his wife to let her know. Without his call, his pasta would not be al dente. Amazing.

I just have a short afternoon to discover Geneva, capital of the canton of Geneva. On the lake, Lake Geneva, a huge geyser! Strange. I go closer to cool down as the temperature is close to 30° Celsius.

In the evening, I eat out outside in the centre of the centre, the Plainpalais plain. I am surprised by the quality of the local wine. I dare to try the chef's special of the day: frogs sautéed with garlic. Yes, you read that right: frogs! And we are supposed to be the barbarians!?!

Vaud (VD) – 2 July 2017

On Sunday, a short train ride on schedule to the town of Nyon in the neighbouring canton of Vaud. I have an appointment for brunch by the lake with an old friend of a friend of a friend, Jean-Marc Carterre, a chief technician working for a very famous brand of Swiss watches which I cannot name here. He is punctual, though his overly expensive watch is stuck at 7 a.m. He explains to me in detail how important watches are for Switzerland. He remains as vague as possible with the numbers. Swiss people are known for bank secrecy; I did not realise the same held true for watchmaking secrecy. I get to know some numbers, though. Switzerland exports about 2 million watches per month (second rank worldwide, behind China), which are cumulatively worth one billion euros (first rank worldwide, by far). He goes into detail about counterfeiting. It is a global war. Merciless. Endless. When the time has come to go back to the train station, he generously pays for the brunch with two dark red 30-franc notes. No, I am joking. Swiss banknotes are even more precise and perfect than their watches.

Late afternoon and evening in Lausanne, the capital. Just enough time and barely enough space in my stomach to enjoy the local delicacy, the *papet vaudois*, a harmonious blend of leeks and potatoes, served with cabbage sausage.

Fribourg (FR) – 3 July 2017

I start this first Swiss Monday wandering through the grassy green hills of Gruyère, a heaven for cows. Unsurprisingly, the region's specialities are milk-related: chocolate, cheese, and double cream. Double cream is just twice as good as regular cream. It is thicker and tastier because it contains much more fat. It is at its yummiest on meringues. I indulge.

World-famous Gruyère cheese comes from Gruyère, Switzerland. Gruyère cheese from elsewhere is like non-Icelandic skyr, a pale imitation. Gruyère cheese meets Vacherin cheese in the evening in Fribourg, the capital city of the canton of Fribourg, in a fondue pot shared with a well-known local citizen, Corinne Salbei. She is one of the Seven Wises. That means she has a seat on the executive council of the country, the Federal Council. She will be Swiss President next year, as Switzerland's presidency rotates yearly amongst the Seven Wises. She unveils to me the secret of the success of Swiss politics. In spite of its reputation for slowness, Switzerland moves in a straightforward manner. Slowly, but efficiently, like a turtle. Meanwhile, French, German, Austrian, and Italian rabbits move at a much faster pace, but to the right, to the left, to centre-right, to centre-left, etcetera. Faster, but not straightforward.

Neuchâtel (NE) – 4 July 2017

I am welcomed in Neuchâtel, the capital city of the canton of Neuchâtel, by a UFO! Yes, a little, round, fluorescent-green UFO lands next to my cup of coffee. The UFO is indeed a local delicacy filled with melting chocolate. It tastes awfully good! Carac is its name. I will remember that. Switzerland's reputation for chocolate is deserved. Even the less-fancy-packaged chocolate bar from a random supermarket tastes far superior to any of our own chocolate, too often filled with liquorice.

34° Celsius. Time for a drink in the shade. Beer wise, Iceland has nothing to envy Switzerland. I share a pilsner as tasty as our supermarket low-in-alcohol ones with Nathalie and Mélanie, two Swiss nurses. They suggest I rather try a monaco, which is a mix of tasteless beer, decent lemonade and tasteful grenadine syrup. Much better! We talk about our health systems. They like the fact our medical insurance is free (well, it is paid via the taxes). They dislike Swiss-style compulsory expensive medical insurance. As there are so many providers, people tend to change provider every year to save a few cents. This results in a useless administrative yearly mess. I am not sure that I understand the subtleties of the Swiss system yet. I think we better stick to ours, simpler. Workwise, alas, they tell me they do as many extra hours as our nurses.

Jura (JU) – 5 July 2017

Saint-Martin's Feast is the canton of Jura's equivalent to our *Þorrablót*. In Iceland, sheep and sharks are eaten from tail to tongue. In Jura, same fate for the pigs. Alas for me, Saint-Martin's is celebrated in November. On this Wednesday in July, I have to opt for plan B, or rather for plan C. C for cervelas. I am in Delémont, the capital city of the canton. Cervelas salad with fresh minced onions comes as a starter, and grilled cervelas is served as the main course. It tasted good until I knew about the ingredients. Cervelas is a Swiss sausage made of bacon, veal, beef, and pork meat, all mixed and stuffed in a… zebu intestine! And we are supposed to be the barbarians!?!

I am formally in the Republic and Canton of Jura. Yes, Switzerland, with its four national languages (German, French, Italian, and Romansh), is a puzzle of 26 republics and cantons, each one with its own sense of autonomy, including its own bank, its own police, and its own education system. 26 cantons, 26 systems, 4 national languages with distinct regional accents, how do they understand each other? They don't! That is why it works, according to Jean Bonhaut, the owner of the cervelas restaurant, who came for dessert with plan D. D for *damassine*, a local plum brandy with an outstanding taste. Plan D again, please!

Basel-Stadt (BS) – 6 July 2017

The city of Basel is the pharmaceutical capital of Switzerland. The pharmaceutical industry is one of the pillars of the Swiss economy with watch factories and banks, cheese and chocolate factories, and of course the legendary Swiss army knife factories.

Basel is the third most populated city after Zürich and Geneva, with about 200,000 inhabitants.

Basel is first and foremost the hometown of the one and only king of Switzerland. Okay, Switzerland is a federal state born some four centuries after Iceland, in 1291, by wiping out the kings and emperors wandering around, and is led by a President nobody can name, but if you ask randomly in the streets who is the most popular Swiss figure since Wilhelm and his apple, it is Roger and his racket. King Roger, Roger the King, Roger I King of the Swiss, or simply The Master, Roger Federer is adulated by adults and children, men and women, the rich and the poor, in every corner of every canton of the country, no matter which language region you are in. He is the best tennis player on Earth. Fact. Lucky Swiss. At least we have Hafþór, the strongest man on Earth…

Basel, the canton, is the smallest of the 26 with only 37 square-kilometres, and it is indeed only half a canton.

Basel-Landschaft (BL) – 7 July 2017

Basel-Landschaft is half a canton as well. Markus Heuschrecker, a worker in the main library of Liestal, the capital, tells me that Basel was one united canton until 1833, when the citizens and the farmers fought each other to defend their diverging interests, with the division of the canton into two half-cantons as a result.

Switzerland is composed of 26 cantons, 6 of them being half-cantons, making it indeed only 23 cantons. This is reflected in the legislative power of the country. The upper house, called the Council of States, has 46 members, two per full-canton, one per half-canton. 2x20 + 1x6 = 46. The lower house has 200 members, elected according to the population of the cantons. Zürich, the most populated, has 34 members. The less populated cantons or half-cantons have 1 member. The executive power, the Federal Council, is composed of the Seven Wises, elected according to a magic formula even our smartest elves would not understand. I will not try to understand it. On the other hand, I do understand that if 100,000 Swiss citizens sign a text, it can become a law. They could forbid pineapples on pizzas by law, for example.

Otherwise, there is nothing worthy of mention in Liestal, apart from a nice fountain near the church.

Aargau (AG) – 8 July 2017

It is Saturday. I wander around the charming old town of Aarau, capital of the canton of Aargau. I try for lunch a typical and delicious Swiss pasta plate, pasta made with fresh eggs called spätzli, with mushrooms.

I have a deep and energic talk with my two neighbours about electricity. They tell me nuclear energy, very present in Aargau, will be abandoned in less than a generation. Oliver Nikkel and Gilles Krome are geothermal engineers. Their job is to convince Swiss citizens how efficient and green geothermal energy is. That is a big challenge, considering the current popularity of windmills and the bright image enjoyed by solar panel sellers. I suggest they move to Iceland, a heaven for geothermal engineers with no need to convince the population. They will think about it. They say that anyway hydraulic energy from the dams is still by far the number one provider of electricity in Switzerland, though global warming could change the situation if glaciers do disappear.

At coffee time, I am a bit surprised that the waiter has no clue what I am talking about when I ask him for a *Sviss Mokka*. It reminds me of Berlin where I could not find Berliner doughnuts, and of Vienna where there were no Vienna sausages to be found.

SOLOTHURN (SO) – 9 JULY 2017

Second Swiss Sunday. Formally Second Sunday in the Swiss Confederation, known to the Latinists as *Confœderatio Helvetica*, hence the CH on the Swiss car plates and as the extension for Swiss websites.

Solothurn, capital of the canton of... Solothurn. Neither the first nor the last canton whose capital bears the same name. Aar River goes through Solothurn, coming from Bern, going to Aargau and Aarau which are named after it. Solothurn's Hauptgasse, its main pedestrian street, is displaying fine examples of Swiss baroque architecture.

I am more and more impressed by the public transport network of the country, its density, its efficiency. A carless (but not careless) life is conceivable in Switzerland.

Curiously, the pharmacy network is as dense as the public transport network. Unsurprisingly, the post office network is as sparse as in Höfuðborgarsvæðið (Greater Reykjavík).

For each new day, one new bread. Yes, every canton has its own. And two or three yoghurts with a new flavour a day keep the doctor away. Diversity is good. A diversity alas unknown at 64° North.

Bern (BE) – 10 July 2017

The city of Bern is the capital of the canton of Bern. Once more. And it has been the capital city of Switzerland since 1848. Both the Swiss government and the parliament are in Bern. The Federal Supreme Court of Switzerland is in Lausanne.

I meet Urs near the Bärengraben (Bear Pit) where bears were but are no longer. Bern's bears now live in the BärenPark, a much more comfortable place for these big brown beasts. One of the bears is called Björk. Urs Zimmermann, the man talking to me about the bears, does not know if it is a tribute to Iceland. What he knows is that bears have been important in Bern for centuries. Precisely since 1191 when Berthold V, Duke of Zähringen, founded the city. He was a bear hunter. Urs Zimmermann is married to Ursula Zimmerfrau, who stands next to him. They talk for me in the local dialect, *Bärndütsch*, one of the many variations of what is commonly called Swiss German. I don't understand a word. They admit to me they do not understand Swiss German speakers from other cantons! That is why Swiss Germans use standard German in writing rather than dialect, although some books have been "translated" in *Bärndütsch*, like Tintin, renamed Täntän. Local bears speak *Bärendütsch*.

Obwalden (OW) – 11 July 2017

And one more half-canton. Obwalden + Nidwalden = Unterwalden. In 1291, Unterwalden, with Schwyz and Uri, founded the original Swiss Confederation. I am precisely in Sarnen, the capital of Obwalden. It is Tuesday.

I spend the afternoon in a pub with a band of Swiss soldiers busy defending the country, their assault rifles aligned in the grass, jass cards in one hand, beer in the other. They explain to me the importance of jass for the unity of the army and the country, as it is the most popular card game in Switzerland, no matter the language. About Swiss beer, they pretend it contains all the cereals and vitamins they need to be fit for fighting. The owner of the pub admits that without the regular presence of the soldiers in his place, he would be bankrupt. Many other pubs depend on the regular presence of Swiss soldiers to stay open. Concerning the expensive outfits of the Swiss soldiers, they are vital to the survival of the factories producing expensive outfits for the Swiss soldiers. It makes sense. Concerning the fighter jets of the Swiss army, not made in Switzerland, nobody could tell me how they contribute to saving the country. Furthermore, they are allowed to fly only during office hours, according to the lieutenant in charge. God save the Swiss.

Nidwalden (NW) – 12 July 2017

Wednesday. I am in Stans, capital of the half-canton of Nidwalden, the other half of Unterwalden. Stans is the hometown of Arnold von Winkelried, legendary defenseman of the Swiss halberd national team. His bravery prevented the Habsburg from equalising in the stoppage time in 1386 in Sempach, securing Switzerland's place in the Nations League for many centuries to come.

Switzerland became united sportively, staying desperately disunited culturally. I am made aware of that paradox by Kevin von Winkelried, not-yet-legendary defenseman of FC Stans, in front of the statue of his glorious ancestor in the town centre. Each linguistic region feels indeed way closer culturally to its big neighbouring country speaking the same language than to the rest of Switzerland: the German-speaking part with Germany, the French-speaking part with France, and the Italian-speaking part with Italy. Sports wise, on the other hand, Switzerland is fully cheering for King Roger, as well as for the football and ice hockey national teams, among others. Kevin does not fail to mention the curling national teams, many times world and Olympic champions. Should we try curling on our frozen lakes in winter?

Lucerne (LU) – 13 July 2017

I spend the full day in the capital of the canton of Lucerne, surprisingly named Lucerne, on the shores of Lake… Lucerne. Well, French speakers name it *Lac des Quatre-Cantons*, Italian speakers *Lago dei Quattro Cantoni*, and Romansch speakers *Lai dals Quatter Chantuns*. Locals name it *Vierwaldstättersee*.

The scenery is somewhere between outstanding and idyllic. Surrounded by high alpine mountains, the lake reminds me of a fjord from our West, except for it is a lake, not a sea. No sea, no fjord. And here, cows reign. By us, sheep are the masters of the hills. The majesty of the landscape is something we obviously share with Switzerland.

Switzerland, in spite of its uninhabited alpine summits and an area only half of Iceland, has 24 times more inhabitants than we do. Switzerland: 8 million inhabitants, Iceland: 330,000. If Iceland is a geographical island, Switzerland is a political one, lost in the middle of the European Union Ocean. Squeezed between Switzerland and the European Union stands Liechtenstein, but that is another story.

I wander endlessly on the charming wooden bridge, the Kapellbrücke, until the sun sets behind the mountains. I am feeling like in a postcard.

Uri (UR) – 14 July 2017

Early morning start from Lucerne to the canton of Uri, on the other shore of *Vierwaldstättersee*. The boat is on time and starts the crossing at 8:11 a.m. I cannot stop enjoying the landscape onboard the *Vierwaldstätterseeschifffahrt* (in English: a cruise on Lake Lucerne), yes, with three "f"s in a row. I catch a glimpse of Switzerland's most famous meadow, Rütli meadow, where the first Swiss gathered more than seven centuries ago to figure out how to kick the ass of the Habsburg family. With success.

I dock in Flüelen, then head to Altdorf, the capital of the canton of Uri, where I come head to head with a statue of Wilhelm Tell and his son Walter. Wilhelm was brave enough to provoke on purpose the Habsburg's authority but unlucky enough to get caught and forced to shoot an apple on his son's head with his crossbow to save his life and his son's life. Myth, fact or fake news, Schiller made a play of it, and Rossini an opera. I think Wilhelm Tell is as real as our saga heroes. According to the Japanese tourists taking many photos of the statue, he would be a perfect manga hero. According to the second group of Japanese tourists, there is a manga hero named *Wolfsmund*, inspired by Wilhelm Tell's saga.

Schwyz (SZ) – 15 July 2017

As soon as I arrive at Schwyz's train station, I notice how the flag of the canton, Schwyz, is strangely similar in its upper left-hand corner to the Swiss flag, and the name Schwyz itself is strangely close to *Schweiz*, which is the German word for Switzerland. Victor Wenger, head of the station, confirms the close links and their historic roots. He is then keen to talk to me about the local star, the world-famous Swiss army knife, as the main factory is in Schwyz. They are proud of it, the Swiss. They won wars thanks to it, according to Victor. The Burgundians even lost a war against the Swiss before fighting it. Schwyz's knife makers sold them a special version of the knife just before the hostilities, a version that came with a wine-bottle-opener option. Burgundians got lost in the Jura forest and never reached Switzerland. There is no mention of that fact in history books, but Victor seems very convinced about it. He even tells me, as I am Icelandic, that they sold to the Vikings another special version of the Swiss army knife, one with a beer-bottle-opener. The Vikings never reached the shores of Switzerland with their Drakkar ships. There is indeed no mention of any Drakkar ship reaching the coasts of Switzerland in history books.

I wander around Schwyz, the town, listening to the peaceful sound of cowbells.

Zug (ZG) – 16 July 2017

Zug's train station is probably the most gleaming of the country. Zug, capital of the canton of Zug. Zug meaning train in German, no wonder they have such a station. Zug has a very advantageous tax system, according to the waiter who brings me the bill for an extra small espresso: 5 Swiss francs! I could get ten coffees for that price in his native island, Sicily. Quality of life comes at a high price, but as a native of Reykjavík, I am not shocked.

Zug, the town, is on the shores of Zug, the lake (*Zugersee*), a lake with a mini geyser, although not as impressive as the big one in Geneva.

Zug is mainly Catholic. Its neighbour Zürich is mainly Protestant. Each canton has its favourite religion, which is either Catholicism or Protestantism. Believe it or not, this has led to armed conflicts between the cantons. The Wars of Kappel took place in 1529 and 1531. Kappel is located close to the Zug-Zürich border. Swiss civil wars are hard to imagine nowadays. That said, the First War of Kappel got solved peacefully around a milk soup! The Second War of Kappel was more bloody than milky, with some 600 victims, mostly on the Protestant defeated side. Among them, reformed theologian Ulrich Zwingli.

ZÜRICH (ZH) – 17 JULY 2017

Midway between Zug and Zürich, not far from Kappel, the train brakes unexpectedly until it stops. The conductor informs the passengers about an "accident of person", in other words, somebody committed suicide. My neighbours are not surprised. They say more than 100 people per year throw themselves desperately under a train in Switzerland. A paradox in one of the happiest countries in the world. Money cannot buy happiness…

However, money can make some people happy for sure. The noisy herd of bankers having lunch next to me on the shores of Lake Zürich, in the city of Zürich, capital of the canton of Zürich, seems more than happy enjoying a sushi lunch with a glass of Bordeaux. They are as noisy as the cows in Schwyz, despite having a tie instead of a bell around their necks. They switch effortlessly between *Züritüütsch*, their dialect, German, and English to communicate with me. I manage to make their feelings switch every minute. Annoyance: by questioning the ethics of Swiss banking secrecy. Astonishment: by mentioning the imprisonment of crooked bankers in Iceland. Embarrassment: by reminding them of the use of deceased Jews' assets by the Swiss banks after the end of the Second World War. Laughter: by revealing the soon-to-be-legalized idea of equal pay for men and women in Icelandic companies.

Schaffhausen (SH) – 18 July 2017

It is just a few minutes after my arrival in Schaffhausen, the capital city of the canton of Schaffhausen, that the secret behind the success of Swiss banks is unveiled to me. In the trolleybus from the railway station to my hotel, a group of left-wing students divulge to me discreetly that Swiss real bank secrecy is to take care of everybody's money, no questions asked. Good people, bad people, ugly people, philanthropists, dictators, pop stars, popes, stars, etc. That way, in case of war, both sides are likely to have their money in a Swiss bank. And nobody wants to bomb his bank account. QED. Thanks, girls.

My afternoon in Schaffhausen gives me the opportunity to chat with a group of German tourists hunting for oriel windows in the old town. They love unusual architecture, and I agree with them: these oriel windows are simply superb. We should think about oriel windows in Iceland. They might fit well with our *gluggaveður*.

In the evening, boudin with apples and rabbit with carrots, plus a Swiss cheese plate, with delicious and tasty bread and jams for dessert. Swiss cuisine is surprising me day after day with its freshness and its diversity.

Thurgau (TG) – 19 July 2017

Believe it or not, the capital of the canton of Thurgau is not Thurgau, but Frauenfeld. Finally, some originality in this country. Literally, Frauenfeld means Field of Women. In the fields, I see only apples and pears, no women. Thurgau's speciality is cider, made from apples and from pears. I stare endlessly at the apple and pear trees in this Eden in the middle of Europe that is Switzerland.

East of Thurgau stands Lake Constance, named after the town of Constance. It acts as a border between Switzerland, Germany, and Austria. German-speaking people call it *Bodensee*. They call Lake Geneva *Genfersee*. Inverted logic. Albert Youngobst, a fisherman, admits after two pints of pear cider that the logic is different in the German part of Switzerland. He makes me aware of the *Röstigraben*, literally the Rift of Rösti, rösti being a plate of hashed potatoes mixed with cheese. In Romandie, the French-speaking part of Switzerland, they call *Röstigraben Barrière de Rösti*, literally Fence of Rösti. Should we put the fence in the rift? *Röstigraben* is a virtual language and cultural border between the French and German parts of Switzerland. In the evening, I indulge in a huge portion of rösti on the shores of *Bodensee*, with an umpteenth pint of pear cider.

Appenzell Ausserrhoden (AR) – 20 July 2017

Appenzell Ausserrhoden and Appenzell Innerrhoden were only one canton, Appenzell, until 1597, when Catholics and Protestants decided to cut the pear in two and split Appenzell into two half-cantons, one Rhode each, the Rhode being a type of territorial subdivision dating from the Middle Ages.

I spend the day in Herisau, the capital of Appenzell Ausserrhoden, the Protestant one. In this half-canton, people voted by raising one of their hands in the town's main square in a meeting called *Landsgemeinde* until 1997.

I taste the two specialities that are typical to the two half-cantons of Appenzell: Appenzeller and Appenzeller. Appenzeller is a cheese made of cow milk, full-bodied, refined with an ultra-secret herbal blend. A delight. Appenzeller, on the other hand, is an alcoholic drink, full-bodied, refined with an ultra-secret herbal blend. Another delight. There is nothing like enjoying a glass of Appenzeller with a slice of Appenzeller or a slice of Appenzeller with a glass of Appenzeller. No doubt that their ultra-secret herbal blends are safely kept safe in the safe of a Swiss bank.

Appenzell Innerrhoden (AI) – 21 July 2017

Friday. Time for a quick jump from Protestant to Catholic Rhode. I reach Appenzell, capital of the half-canton of Appenzell Innerrhoden.

Apart from lovely wooden houses with exquisite flowers on their balconies, and from a garden gnome shop, there is nothing worth mentioning in Appenzell.

I chat on a public bench with Rosa Schwarz-Weiss, one of the first women who was given the right to vote in this remote corner of Switzerland, a right to vote imposed in 1990 by the Swiss Confederation to the men of the local *Landsgemeinde* after they refused to give women that right not once, not twice, but three times. Appenzell Innerrhoden was the last canton where women were not allowed to vote. Icelandic women can vote since 1915. Rosa Schwarz-Weiss maliciously tells me that times are changing. Now women can vote and are entitled to a rather generous 14-week maternity leave; meanwhile, men are entitled to a rather ridiculous 1-day paternity leave, 90 days less than Icelandic men.

To say that Switzerland is quite far behind Scandinavia (Finland and Iceland included) on the issue of parental leave is a polite understatement.

St. Gallen (SG) – 22 July 2017

This Saturday in St. Gallen, capital of the canton of St. Gallen, starts with a big frog in my throat. I don't understand. I indulged in enough Appenzeller (the drink) to kill every single evil bacterium to be found between my mouth and my stomach. A visit to the majestic Abbey Cathedral of Saint Gall, founded in 613 and named after the Irish monk Gallus, aka Saint Gall, gives me the chance to kick the frog out of my throat. I meet Ben Gall, an Irish monk, not a saint yet. He studies in St. Gallen and masters Swiss German pretty well. He strongly recommends me to say out loud *Chuchichäschtli*. It means *eldhússkápur* in Icelandic and kitchen cabinet in English. The main interest of *Chuchichäschtli* is its pronunciation. Ben makes me say it correctly five times in a row, and here we go, the frog is gone! Try it for yourself: five times *Chuchichäschtli*, no frogs anymore, guaranteed!

Frog out, sausage in. I savour the other star among Swiss sausages with cervelas, *St. Galler Kalbsbratwurst*, a veal sausage best enjoyed roasted. It is made only of local veal, bacon, and… milk. Yes, even sausages are dairy products in the dairy heaven of Switzerland.

GLARUS (GL) – 23 JULY 2017

Glarus is a canton with an impressive alpine background; a perfect place to bring our politicians for winter holidays.

A Sunday in Glarus, capital of the canton of… Glarus. Okay, I counted. 14 out of 26 cantons have the same name as their capital.

A Sunday in Glarus, well, most shops are closed. I wander around admiring the alpine background. A passing passer-by tells me that the sports shop of the local star, alpine ski racer Vreni Schneider, is closed too. It is specialized in winter sports anyway, and we are in July. Born in Elm, in the southern part of the canton, Vreni Schneider won five Winter Olympics medals (three of them gold) and six Alpine World Ski Championships medals (three of them gold). This is indeed five more medals than Iceland at the Winter Olympics, and six more at the Alpine World Ski Championships. Well done, Vreni!

Glarus in the summertime… its alpine landscape and alphorn melodies in the background. Lovely atmosphere. Alphorn melodies, along with cowbell melodies, are the only ones popular on both sides of the *Röstigraben*.

Liechtenstein (FL) – 24 July 2017

I leave Swiss inferno for a day. I don't mean inferno for the above 30° Celsius temperatures. I mean inferno because, in Icelandic, the word for inferno is *helvíti*, which sounds to me like the second word of the Latin name of Switzerland, *Confoederatio Helvetica*.

Liechtenstein is a small principality stuck between Austria and Switzerland. It does not take me long to visit the capital, Vaduz, and its 5,500 inhabitants. Liechtenstein's population is about 40,000, less than the Faroe Islands or Greenland, eight times less than Iceland.

I spot the castle of the Prince, high up on a hill. The current Prince is Johannes Adam Ferdinand Alois Josef Maria Marko d'Aviano Pius, aka Hans Adam II. To be precise, he holds the titles of *Fürst von und zu Liechtenstein, Herzog von Troppau und Jägerndorf, Graf zu Rietberg, Regierer des Hauses von und zu Liechtenstein.* He is the son of Franz Josef Maria Aloys Alfred Karl Johannes Heinrich Michael Georg Ignatius Benediktus Gerhardus Majella, aka Franz-Josef II, and Georgina Norberta Johanna Franziska Antonie Marie Raphaela von Wilczek, aka Gina. Good that we got rid of the monarchy, our names are already complicated enough to explain to foreigners. And we do not even have family names.

Grisons (GR) – 25 July 2017

Back to Switzerland on this Tuesday. More precisely in Chur, capital of the canton of Grisons, the largest Swiss canton, representing one-sixth of the country. As in Glarus, the alpine background is outstanding.

The only National Park of Switzerland is in Grisons. Only one. We have three. For countries fond of beautiful landscapes, that sounds little. We can do better.

Grisons is where Romansh is spoken, the fourth national language after German, French, and Italian. About 60,000 people speak Romansh. More people speak Faroese. Romansh is under permanent threat by its big neighbouring languages, German and Italian. Furthermore, Romansh is subdivided into five distinct dialects: Vallader, Putèr, Surmiran, Sursilvan, and Sutsilvan. I wish Romansh speakers good luck in preserving their language and dialects, or *buna fortuna*, as they say in Romansh.

To end the day in style, I savour a plate of dried beef meat, which is sooo much more succulent than our dried fishes. With the coffee comes a thick piece of yummissimo walnut pie.

Ticino (TI) – 26 July 2017

No direct train between Grisons and Ticino. I opt for a spectacular bus ride from Chur to Bellinzona. A pleasure for the eyes, a torture for the stomach. Too much walnut pie for breakfast…

Bellinzona is the capital of Canton Ticino, a mostly Italian-speaking canton. About 6% of the Swiss population speaks Italian. 64% speaks German, and 21% French. Romansh is spoken by less than 1%. Okay, mathematicians: 64 + 21 + 6 + 1 = 92. What about the remaining 8%? They speak another language, like Albanian, Portuguese, Spanish, Serbian and Croatian, or English. Note that all the aforementioned languages represent more than 1% of the Swiss population. In Iceland, apart from Icelandic, only Polish is spoken by more than 1% of the population. Switzerland is by far more multicultural than Iceland. I learn these interesting numbers from the mouth of Cederico Enrico Roseroni, a prominent statistician and the first assistant of the Mayor of Bellinzona. He invites me to share a polenta in the evening, which comes along with a perfectly braised beef tenderloin and a Merlot with subtle notes of blueberry. Delightful! Switzerland has been smart to borrow some delicacies from its gastronomically renowned neighbours, allowing its visitors to indulge in more than the ubiquitous fondue.

Valais (VS) – 27 July 2017

Last on my list, the canton of Valais. A bilingual canton, like Fribourg. Its best-known symbol is the Matterhorn, a mountain top that symbolizes alone the beauty of the Alps. That is for the German-speaking side. The French-speaking side is known almost worldwide for its Valais Fair in Martigny and its Carnival in Monthey. The capital, Sion, is famous for its football team, FC Sion, a legendary team that managed to win its first 13 Swiss Cup finals. You read that right: 13/13, like the number of stars on the Valais flag. Amazing!

I am very lucky to be able to fly over the Matterhorn and the Gornergrat rocky ridge with local star pilot Roland Maximus and his teammate-for-the-day Olivier Duhlac, usually busy racing with a monohull on Lake Geneva.

After a spectacular flight, it is *apéro* time on the terrace of Sion airport. Cornalin, a native grape variety of Valais, fills our glasses with its subtle notes of black cherry. We indulge in an *assiette valaisanne*, a plate from the region filled with bacon, dried beef meat, raw ham, rye bread, alpine cheese, and dry sausage.

In the evening, I taste *raclette* in its purest version: half an alpine cheese wheel melted with the soft flame of a wood fire. And the white wines that go with it. Sublime!

EPILOGUE

Álftanes, Iceland, 15 August 2017

Sigmundur Sig Sigmundsson is back home. He brought back some clues about how to make Iceland great again, greater than Switzerland, higher on Dubreuil's Ranking, the most reliable quality-of-life country ranking in the world, possibly at rank number one.

President Ragnar Gnarr Gnarrson, Prime Minister Arndís Rós Björksdóttir, LGBT and Culture Minister Ævar Stein Kasperson, Fishery and Agriculture Minister Aðalgeir Gull Björnsson, and of course Football and Foreign Minister Margrét Olga Kristjánsdóttir are all keen to hear Sigmundur Sig again.

At the end of Triple Sig's debriefing, President Gnarrson announces he wants to put in the constitution the principle of a popular initiative to give Icelanders the chance to force a vote on banning pineapples on pizzas.

Prime Minister Arndís Rós reminds everyone that former Swiss President Oskar Pomme is now in jail for having offered a too-fair-to-be-true tax agreement to the Dubreuil family, the organizer of the quality-of-life country ranking. She suggests acting with more tact.

Margrét Olga Kristjánsdóttir is next to speak. She considers moving Iceland's population to Tenerife in the Canary Islands in order to improve food diversity, cultural diversity, and the weather.

Fishery and Agriculture Minister Aðalgeir Gull wants Iceland to be closer to the European market by building a mega-bridge and a mega-tunnel to the continent.

Sigmundur Sig sums up the meeting. He says it would be good to focus on the diversification of the food offered by building more greenhouses and on the improvement of the public transportation network, notably outside Reykjavík. With geothermal energy and cheap electricity, these challenges seem feasible. He recommends following Norway's leadership on electric cars. And that's all, folks, he tells a captive audience, as Iceland is far ahead of Switzerland regarding education and welfare. Military wise, he advises staying without an army, advocating rather to invest more in research and healthcare.

President Gnarrson takes note of Sigmundur's smart considerations and swears to bring them personally to the Parliament to make sure they turn quickly into actions.

APPENDIX

A1. Historical Accession to the Swiss Confederation

1291: Uri, Schwyz, Obwalden, Nidwalden

1332: Lucerne

1351: Zürich

1352: Zug, Glarus

1353: Bern

1481: Fribourg, Solothurn

1501: Basel-Landschaft, Basel-Stadt, Schaffhausen

1513: Appenzell Ausserrhoden,

Appenzell Innerrhoden

1803: St. Gallen, Aargau, Grisons,

Thurgau, Ticino, Vaud

1815: Valais, Neuchâtel, Geneva

1979: Jura

2066: Liechtenstein

A2. Train Travel Times between the Capitals

Geneva (GE) – Lausanne (VD): 36 minutes

Lausanne (VD) – Fribourg (FR): 43 minutes

Fribourg (FR) – Neuchâtel (NE): 53 minutes

Neuchâtel (NE) – Delémont (JU): 49 minutes

Delémont (JU) – Basel (BS): 30 minutes

Basel (BS) – Liestal (BL): 9 minutes

Liestal (BL) – Aarau (AG): 27 minutes

Aarau (AG) – Solothurn (SO): 27 minutes

Solothurn (SO) – Bern (BE): 50 minutes

Bern (BE) – Sarnen (OW): 84 minutes

Sarnen (OW) – Stans (NW): 29 minutes

Stans (NW) – Lucerne (LU): 15 minutes

Lucerne (LU) – Altdorf (UR): 58 minutes

Altdorf (UR) – Schwyz (SZ): 19 minutes

Schwyz (SZ) – Zug (ZG): 39 minutes

Zug (ZG) – Zürich (ZH): 21 minutes

Zürich (ZH) – Schaffhausen (SH): 36 minutes

Schaffhausen (SH) – Frauenfeld (TG): 49 minutes

Frauenfeld (TG) – Herisau (AR): 69 minutes

Herisau (AR) – Appenzell (AI): 32 minutes

Appenzell (AI) – St. Gallen (SG): 44 minutes

St. Gallen (SG) – Glarus (GL): 72 minutes

Glarus (GL) – Vaduz (FL): 76 minutes (train+bus)

Vaduz (FL) – Chur (GR): 46 minutes (bus+train)

Chur (GR) – Bellinzona (TI): 120 minutes (bus)

Bellinzona (TI) – Sion (VS): 214 minutes

Sion (VS) – Geneva (GE): 94 minutes.

ACKNOWLEDGEMENTS

Thank you to Christina Cutting for having thoroughly proofread this book.

Thanks for their contribution to the project via crowdfunding to: Christophe Bornand, Corinne Sauge, Jean-Marc Errecart, Mélanie Soulier Peci, Michel Bucher, Nathalie Dalberto, Nicolas Summermatter, Olivier Dumont, Roland Millius, Sok Meng Cheng, and Youngo Taramarcaz.

Thanks to Yann Sommer for June 28th, 2021.

ABOUT C.H. ROSERENS

A traveller and a writer, as well as a digital nomad, web content writer, chocoholic, vexillologist, and avid stargazer, CÉDRIC HENRI ROSERENS was born in Martigny, Valais, Switzerland, in 1974. Too late to be James Cook and explore the unknown islands of the Pacific Ocean. Too early to be James Kirk and explore the unknown star systems of the Milky Way.

Cédric Henri Roserens is the self-published author of FANTASVISS *and* HAPPÍSLAND *(short stories),* UNCLE GREG'S TREASURE *(novel),* PLANET ASPERGER *(miniguide) and* LONGITUDE 360 *(haikus). He also collaborated on the collection of short stories* LA FEMME EST L'AVENIR DE L'HOMME *(Éditions Montsalvens).*